Bassoon / Trombone / Euphonium BC/TC

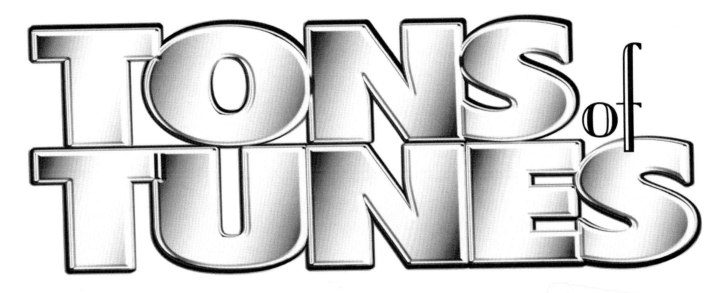

FOR CHURCH

AMY ADAM
MIKE HANNICKEL

CURNOW®
MUSIC

EXCLUSIVELY DISTRIBUTED BY

HAL•LEONARD®
CORPORATION
7777 W. BLUEMOUND RD. P.O. BOX 13819 MILWAUKEE, WI 53213

CD number: 19-047-3 CMP

CD arrangements by James L. Hosay

Edition Number: CMP 0875-03-400

Amy Adam, Mike Hannickel

TONS OF TUNES for Church

Bassoon / Trombone / Euphonium BC/TC

ISBN 978-90-431-1979-5

ARRANGERS

MIKE HANNICKEL grew up in the Sacramento, California area and attended California State University, Sacramento and the University of Southern California. He has been a music teacher in Rocklin, California since 1973. He also composes and publishes exclusively with Curnow Music Press, with whom he has dozens of pieces of music in print.

AMY ADAM was raised in Grand Rapids, Minnesota and attended the University of Minnesota, Duluth graduating with a BM in band education and Flute performance. She has been a music teacher in California since 1992 and currently teaches in Rocklin, California.

TONS OF TUNES

TONS OF TUNES FOR CHURCH is filled with fun and familiar pieces that musicians love to play. All the songs have been arranged in easy keys for wind instruments. The **professional quality accompaniment CD** can be used for practice and performance. You may also choose to purchase the separately available Piano accompaniment part.

TO THE MUSIC TEACHER OR CHURCH MUSIC DIRECTOR:
TONS OF TUNES for CHURCH is a great way to help get young musicians actively involved in your church music program. Every tune in the book can be performed with the included CD accompaniment or with the separately available Piano/Organ book. All **TONS OF TUNES for CHURCH** books can be used alone or together so a variety of small ensembles can be created. Whether for prelude, offertory, church social, talent show or any other gathering, **TONS OF TUNES for CHURCH** is just what you need. Chord symbols are provided in the Piano accompaniment book for Keyboard, Guitar and combo use.

TO THE MUSICIAN:
Have **FUN** playing these songs alone or with your family and friends! Even if you have different instruments, you can still play together. Each person needs to get the **TONS OF TUNES FOR CHURCH** book for their instrument.

11. COME, THOU ALMIGHTY KING

12. OH, WON'T YOU SIT DOWN?

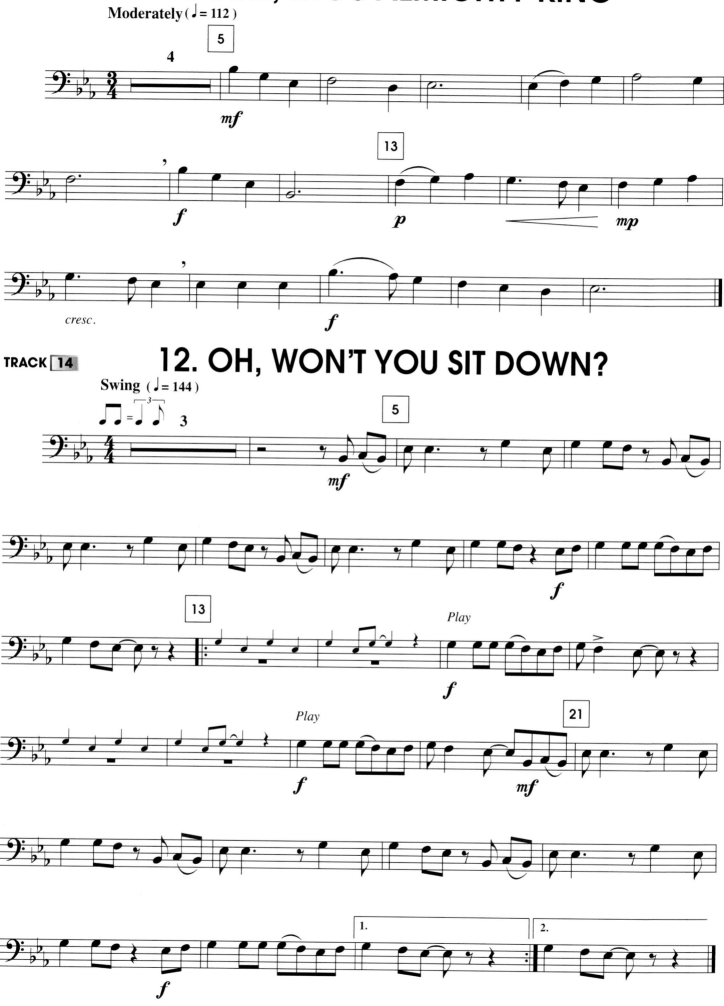

0875.03 CMP • Bassoon / Trombone / Euphonium BC/TC

ARRANGERS

MIKE HANNICKEL grew up in the Sacramento, California area and attended California State University, Sacramento and the University of Southern California. He has been a music teacher in Rocklin, California since 1973. He also composes and publishes exclusively with Curnow Music Press, with whom he has dozens of pieces of music in print.

AMY ADAM was raised in Grand Rapids, Minnesota and attended the University of Minnesota, Duluth graduating with a BM in band education and Flute performance. She has been a music teacher in California since 1992 and currently teaches in Rocklin, California.

TONS OF TUNES

TONS OF TUNES FOR CHURCH is filled with fun and familiar pieces that musicians love to play. All the songs have been arranged in easy keys for wind instruments. The **professional quality accompaniment CD** can be used for practice and performance. You may also choose to purchase the separately available Piano accompaniment part.

TO THE MUSIC TEACHER OR CHURCH MUSIC DIRECTOR:
TONS OF TUNES for CHURCH is a great way to help get young musicians actively involved in your church music program. Every tune in the book can be performed with the included CD accompaniment or with the separately available Piano/Organ book. All **TONS OF TUNES for CHURCH** books can be used alone or together so a variety of small ensembles can be created. Whether for prelude, offertory, church social, talent show or any other gathering, **TONS OF TUNES for CHURCH** is just what you need. Chord symbols are provided in the Piano accompaniment book for Keyboard, Guitar and combo use.

TO THE MUSICIAN:
Have **FUN** playing these songs alone or with your family and friends! Even if you have different instruments, you can still play together. Each person needs to get the **TONS OF TUNES FOR CHURCH** book for their instrument.

FOR CHURCH
CONTENTS

TONS OF TUNES FOR CHURCH

TROMBONE
EUPHONIUM B.C.
BASSOON

Amy Adam (ASCAP) and
Mike Hannickel (ASCAP)

1. ABIDE WITH ME

TRACK 3

Moderately (♩ = 116)

2. NOW THANK WE ALL OUR GOD

TRACK 4

Gently (♩ = 108)

TRACK **5**   Cheerfully (♩ = 144)

3. DO, LORD

mf

13

mp

Fine

f *mp* *mf* *mp*

21

p *cresc.* *mp*

29

cresc. *mf* *cresc.*

D.S. al Fine

f *dim.* *mp*

TRACK **6**

4. BEAUTIFUL SAVIOR

Moderately (♩ = 108)

p *mp*

mf *mp*

13

p *mp* *mf*

1. | 2.

p *p*

    0875.03 CMP • Bassoon / Trombone / Euphonium BC/TC

5. FOR THE BEAUTY OF THE EARTH

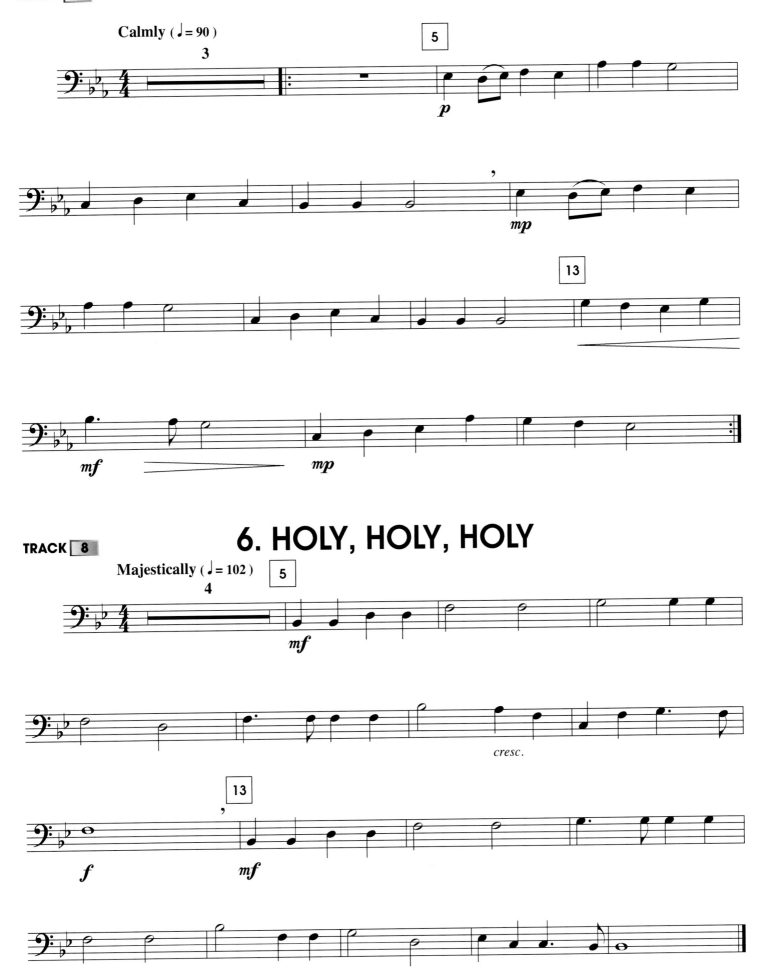

6. HOLY, HOLY, HOLY

7. JESUS LOVES ME

Cheerfully (♩ = 124)

8. MY FAITH LOOKS UP TO THEE

Moderately (♩ = 96)

9. JUST AS I AM

TRACK 11

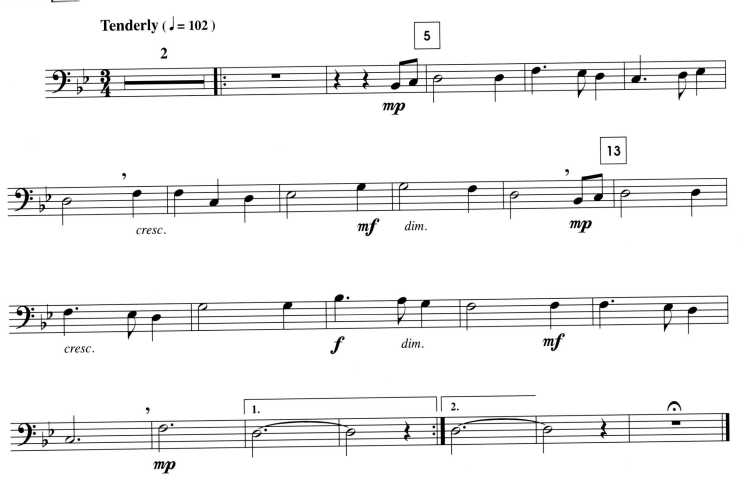

10. CROWN HIM WITH MANY CROWNS

TRACK 12

11. COME, THOU ALMIGHTY KING

Moderately (♩ = 112)

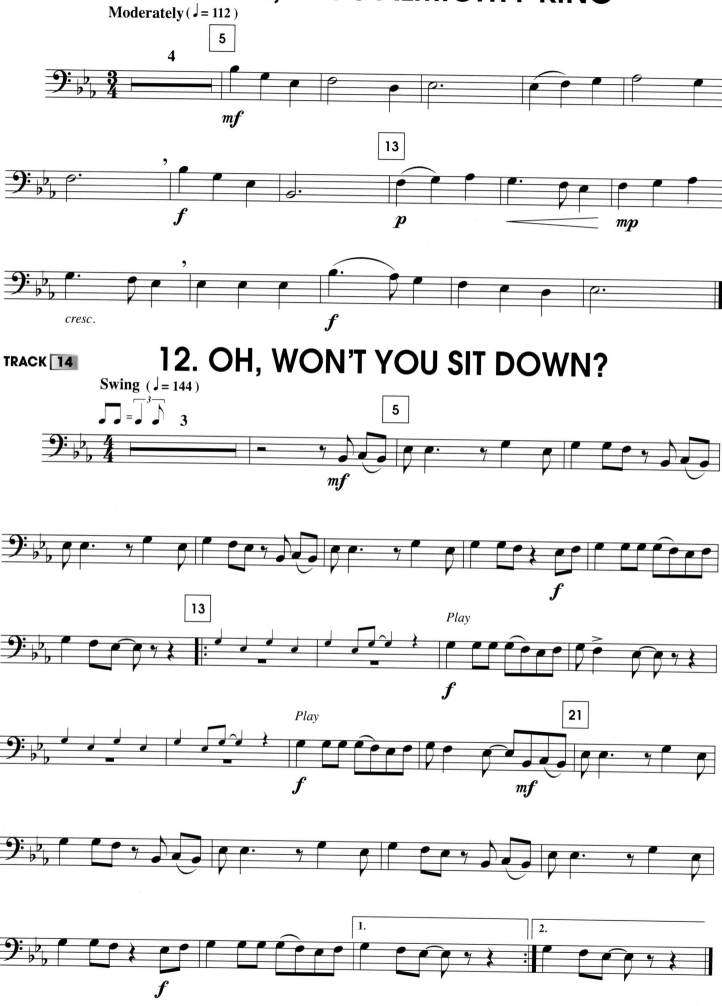

12. OH, WON'T YOU SIT DOWN?

Swing (♩ = 144)

10

13. O FOR A THOUSAND TONGUES

Moderately (♩ = 108)

14. CHILDREN OF THE HEAVENLY FATHER

Lightly (♩ = 102)

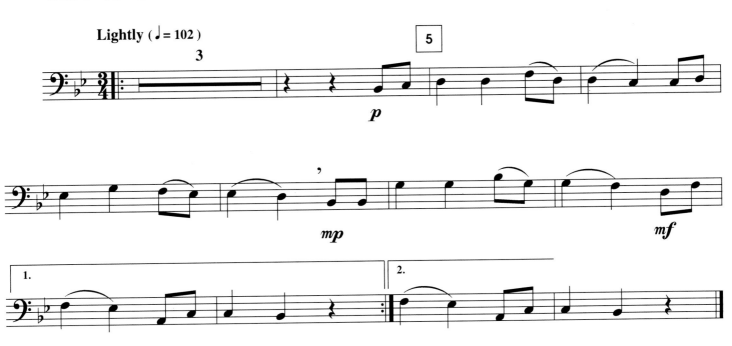

15. THE CHURCH'S ONE FOUNDATION

16. NEARER MY GOD TO THEE

0875.03 CMP • Bassoon / Trombone / Euphonium BC/TC

17. PRAISE TO THE LORD, THE ALMIGHTY

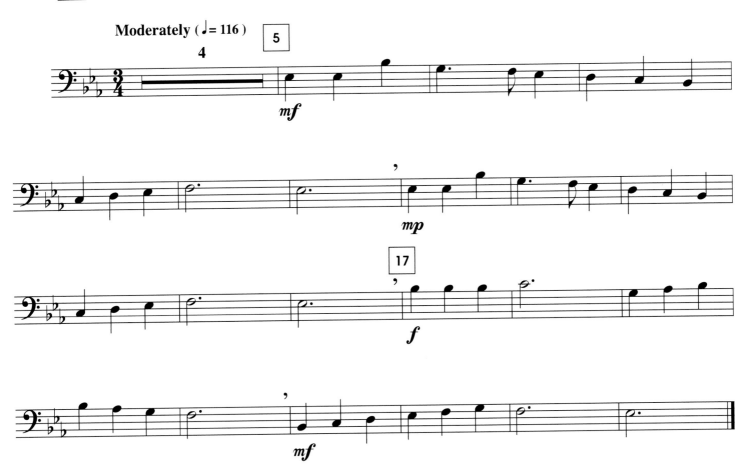

18. ALL GLORY, LAUD AND HONOR

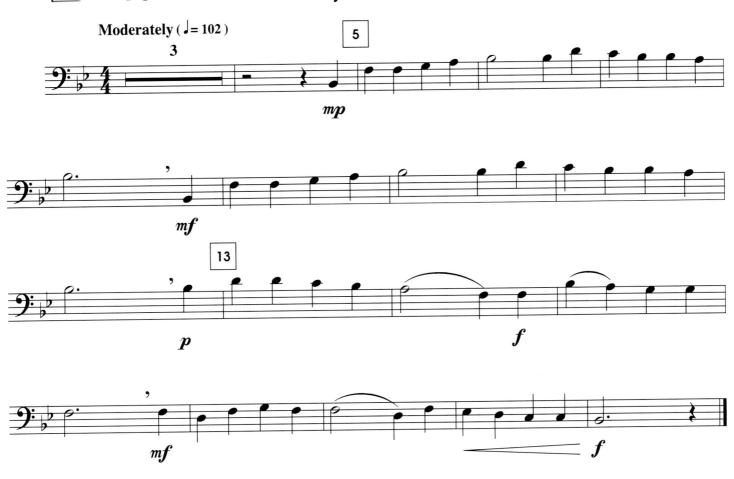

19. ALL HAIL THE POWER

20. GOD OF GRACE AND GOD OF GLORY

14   0875.03 CMP • Bassoon / Trombone / Euphonium BC/TC

21. SWING LOW, SWEET CHARIOT

22. HE'S GOT THE WHOLE WORLD IN HIS HANDS

23. GO TELL IT ON THE MOUNTAIN

24. THIS TRAIN

25. WHAT A FRIEND WE HAVE IN JESUS

26. ONWARD CHRISTIAN SOLDIERS

27. IN THE SWEET BY AND BY

28. LET US BREAK BREAD TOGETHER

0875.03 CMP • Bassoon / Trombone / Euphonium BC/TC

29. CHRIST THE LORD IS RISEN TODAY

30. WERE YOU THERE?

31. THIS IS MY FATHER'S WORLD

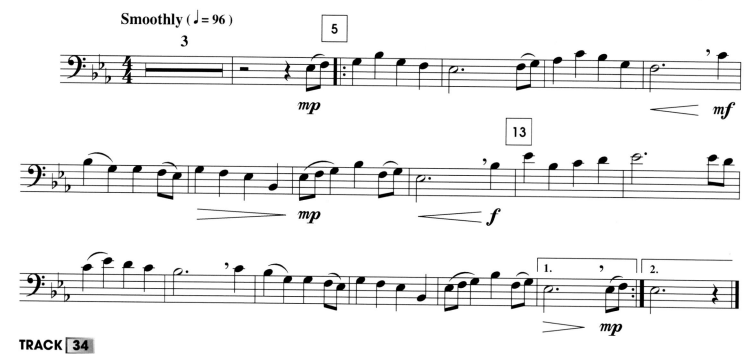

32. SOFTLY AND TENDERLY JESUS IS CALLING

0875.03 CMP • Bassoon / Trombone / Euphonium BC/TC

TONS OF TUNES FOR CHURCH

Amy Adam (ASCAP) and
Mike Hannickel (ASCAP)

1. ABIDE WITH ME

2. NOW THANK WE ALL OUR GOD

3. DO, LORD

4. BEAUTIFUL SAVIOR

0875.03 CMP • Bassoon / Trombone / Euphonium BC/TC

5. FOR THE BEAUTY OF THE EARTH

6. HOLY, HOLY, HOLY

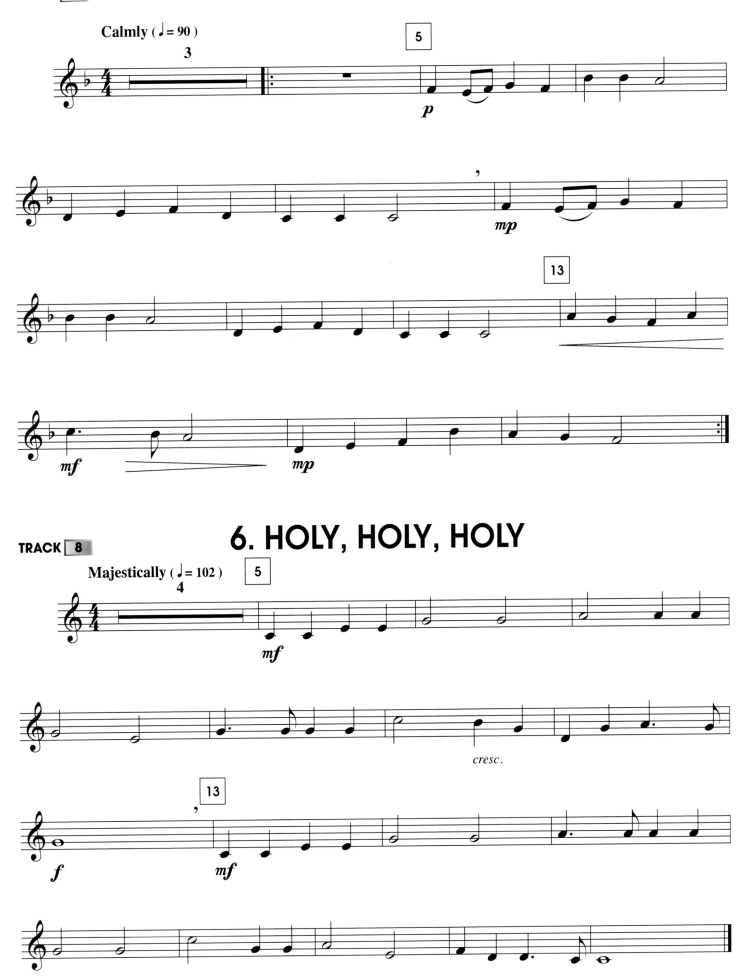

7. JESUS LOVES ME

8. MY FAITH LOOKS UP TO THEE

0875.03 CMP • Bassoon / Trombone / Euphonium BC/TC

9. JUST AS I AM

Tenderly (♩ = 102)

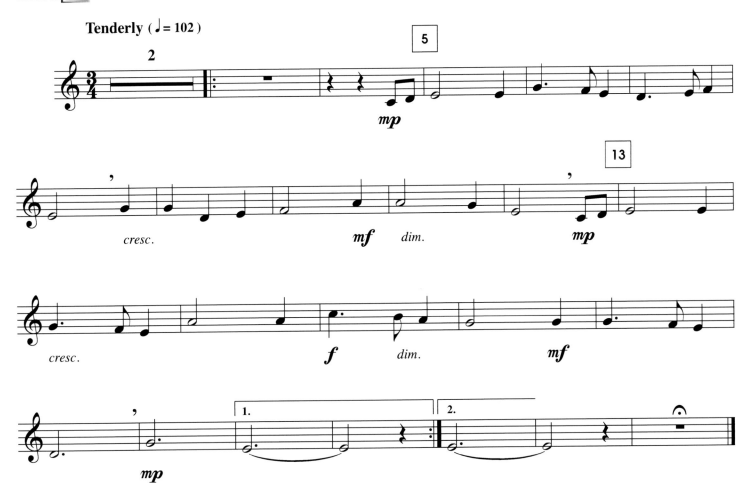

10. CROWN HIM WITH MANY CROWNS

Majestically (♩ = 102)

11. COME, THOU ALMIGHTY KING

12. OH, WON'T YOU SIT DOWN?

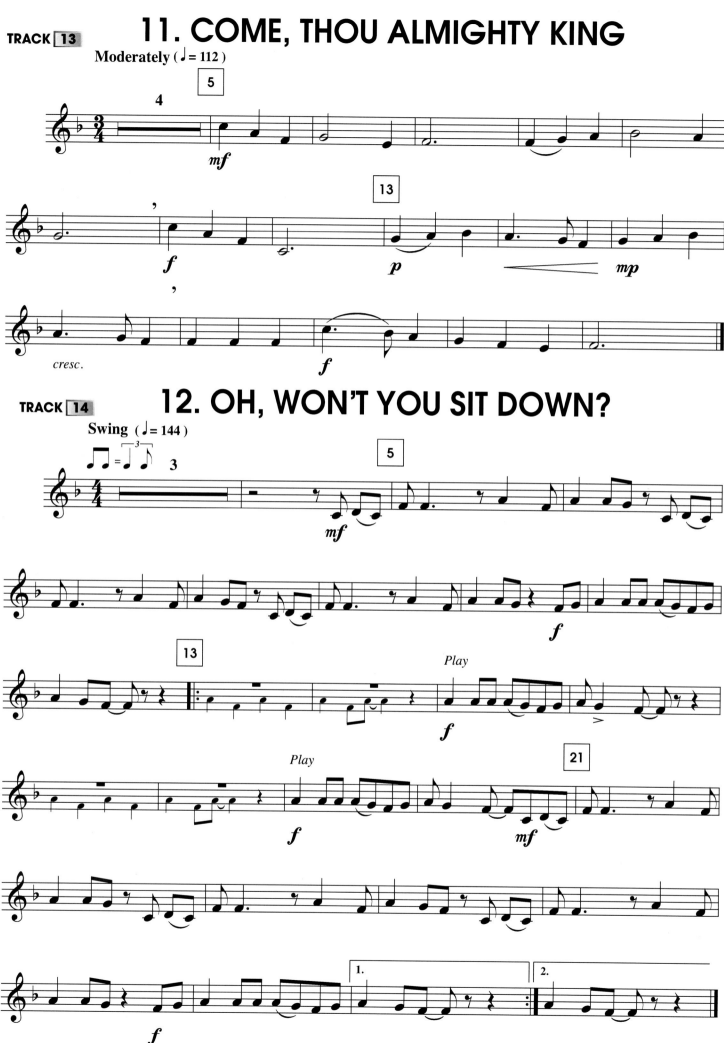

0875.03 CMP • Bassoon / Trombone / Euphonium BC/TC

13. O FOR A THOUSAND TONGUES

14. CHILDREN OF THE HEAVENLY FATHER

15. THE CHURCH'S ONE FOUNDATION

16. NEARER MY GOD TO THEE

17. PRAISE TO THE LORD, THE ALMIGHTY

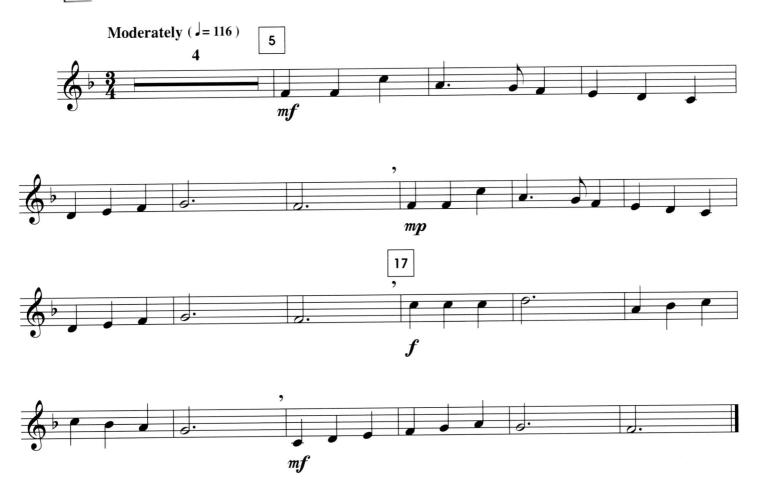

18. ALL GLORY, LAUD AND HONOR

19. ALL HAIL THE POWER

20. GOD OF GRACE AND GOD OF GLORY

0875.03 CMP • Bassoon / Trombone / Euphonium BC/TC

21. SWING LOW, SWEET CHARIOT

22. HE'S GOT THE WHOLE WORLD IN HIS HANDS

23. GO TELL IT ON THE MOUNTAIN

24. THIS TRAIN

27. IN THE SWEET BY AND BY

28. LET US BREAK BREAD TOGETHER

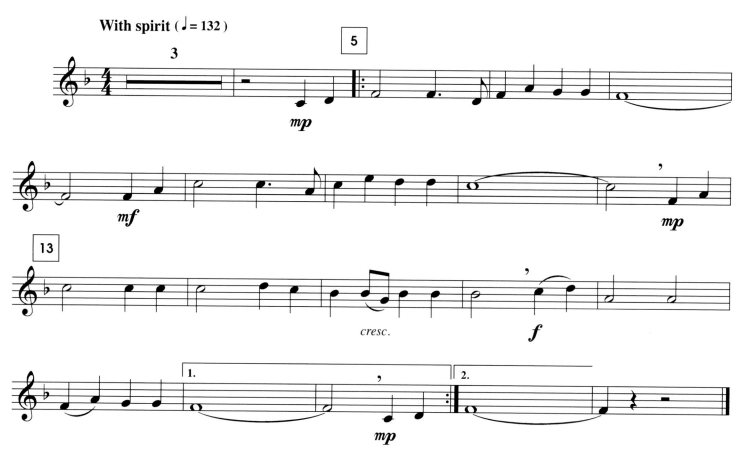

0875.03 CMP • Bassoon / Trombone / Euphonium BC/TC

29. CHRIST THE LORD IS RISEN TODAY

Majestically (♩ = 116)

30. WERE YOU THERE?

Gently (♩ = 76)

31. THIS IS MY FATHER'S WORLD

32. SOFTLY AND TENDERLY JESUS IS CALLING